# THE MIRROR'S BEEN LYING TO YOU

# THE MIRROR'S BEEN LYING TO YOU

## How to Look and Feel Beautiful Every Day

### SHER CANADA

NAPLES, FL

Copyright © 2026 by Sher Canada
All rights reserved.

Published in the United States by
O'Leary Publishing
www.olearypublishing.com

The views, information, or opinions expressed in this book are solely those of the authors involved and do not necessarily represent those of O'Leary Publishing, LLC.

The author has made every effort possible to ensure the accuracy of the information presented in this book. However, the information herein is sold without warranty, either expressed or implied. Neither the author, publisher, nor any dealer or distributor of this book will be held liable for any damages caused either directly or indirectly by the instructions or information contained in this book. You are encouraged to seek professional advice before taking any action mentioned herein.

All rights reserved. No part of this book may be reproduced or transmitted in any form by any means: electronic, mechanical, photocopy, recording, or other, without the prior and express written permission of the author, except for brief cited quotes. For information on getting permission for reprints and excerpts, contact: O'Leary Publishing.

ISBN: (print) 978-1-952491-94-8
ISBN: (ebook) 978-1-952491-95-5
LCCN: 202592525

Developmental Editing by Heather Davis Desrocher
Line Editing by Kat Langenheim
Proofreading by Jennifer Doody
Cover and Interior Design by Jessica Angerstein
Author Headshot Courtesy of The Power Project Women Rising, Communities Thriving ©

Printed in the United States of America

To all the amazing women I've worked with
throughout my career,
who taught me to *be* better
and *lead* better than the day before.

Use this QR code to access
Sher's vault of fashion videos.

# Contents

**Preface**  The Mirror's Been Lying to You .................................. 1

**Introduction**  The Style Doctor .................................................. 3

**Chapter 1** | Finding Your Style Uniform ............................... 7

**Chapter 2** | Foolproof Ways to Always Look Stylish .......... 21

**Chapter 3** | Clothing that Goes with Everything ............... 33

**Chapter 4** | Slim Secrets ......................................................... 47

**Chapter 5** | How to Buy Bottoms For Your Rear End ....... 57

**Chapter 6** | The LBD – Little Black Dress .......................... 73

**Chapter 7** | The Shoes that Go with Everything ................ 81

**Chapter 8** | How to Take the Best Photo Ever .................... 91

**Chapter 9** | Closet Clean Out .................................................. 97

**Chapter 10** | Packing Tips and Tricks ................................. 105

**Chapter 11** | The Habits of an Attractive Woman ............. 111

**Chapter 12** | Stop Wearing These Three Things ............... 123

**Chapter 13** | How to Fall in Love With Yourself ................ 127

**Conclusion** ............................................................................... 135

**Acknowledgments** ................................................................. 137

**About the Author** ................................................................... 139

## Preface

# The Mirror's Been Lying to You

I know you have been in this frustrating situation: You are in front of the mirror staring at yourself, ready to head out the door; but you feel like your outfit does **not** present the **best** of **you**. There's no time to change and you don't even know what you'd change into. So, out the door you go, wishing you could do something to feel more comfortable and more confident.

**You** are **not** alone! Every woman has experienced this. But *what if* the mirror has been lying to you? What if every time you look in the mirror you see things that no one else sees? We as women are so critical of ourselves.

We need to **stop**! We need to appreciate what God gave us, find our best features, and dress to showcase them! **You can do this!**

Changing your experience with clothes and getting ready every day is much easier than you think! I am **not** going to call you an apple or a pear or any other sort of fruit. That stuff drives me crazy! I am **not** going to tell you that you can't wear white bottoms after Memorial Day – who said that anyway?

What I am going to do is teach you some easy and simple tips and tricks to look and feel beautiful and confident. *I believe that confidence is the single most beautiful thing a woman can wear every day!* And this book is all about showing you how to wear confidence every single day. My dream is that when you are done reading, you will know how to look and feel more beautiful and confident. Let's dive in!

## Introduction

# The Style Doctor

Over the last 40 years I have spent many hours in the fitting room with clients. It really is the best place to learn! And here is what I have learned: most women look in the mirror and see things that absolutely ***no one else*** sees. Maybe you are a woman who does this? It breaks my heart when a woman looks in the mirror and does not like the image she sees.

Over these many decades of my amazing career in retail at brands such as Brooks Fashions, The Limited, The Wet Seal, Chico's, Soma and Boston Proper, I have learned how to help women have a wonderful experience with their clothes, and a positive relationship with their appearance.

Today, I have my very own boutique in beautiful Naples, Florida. Shecanlove 💋 is a luxury boutique for chic women that exists to uplift, teach and inspire women while offering meticulously curated fashion, tennis, pickleball, golf, and athleisure. We are ***luxury you live in*** and we provide a shopping experience where women feel beautiful and receive superior personal service. We also ship right to your door through **shecanlove.com**.

I *live* for this. I am addicted to fashion – and to helping women look and feel beautiful! It is my superpower. I *never* give up – on any woman. I know that *every* woman can look beautiful in her clothing *if* she makes the right choices for her body type.

The older I am, the more I follow the simple guidelines in this book: classic, fabulous choices for *my* body and *my* lifestyle. Over the years I have established what I look great in, and more importantly what I don't! I promise when you follow the steps outlined in this book you will love looking in the mirror and seeing the fabulous new *you*! Just call me the style doctor!

I want to share all that I know with you, and with as many women as I can. That is my hope for this book. I wrote it for all the women I have styled over the last 40+

years, and for all the women I have not yet met, including you, so that you can look and feel more beautiful every day!

**STYLE IS SOMETHING EACH OF US ALREADY HAS, ALL WE NEED TO DO IS FIND IT.**

-DIANE VON FURSTENBERG

# Chapter 1
# Finding Your Style Uniform

The first step to feeling effortlessly great, and looking more beautiful, is discovering your personal style uniform. Style refers to your particular way of expressing yourself. The first way we come to know someone – even before speaking to them – is to simply look at what they are wearing. We communicate who we are with our wardrobe, which makes developing your personal style even more important. One of the main reasons I chose a career in fashion was because of my fascination with personal style.

A style uniform is a combination of clothing items and accessories that make you look and feel beautiful and *most* like yourself. If you have a go-to outfit combination that you reach for when you don't know what else to wear, then consider that your uniform. There are so many benefits to predictability with your style: from better shopping habits to more confidence. As I will keep telling you: ***the single most beautiful thing a woman can wear every day is confidence.***

You may ask, "Won't I become bored having a uniform?" Well, from my experience, I was bored **until** I started to buy items that really suited my personal style. I'm a jeans, white shirt, blazer and pumps or sneakers kind of girl. Since finding my style uniform, I feel my best, and shopping is easier because I have a lane. I no longer just wander aimlessly around the store.

Great personal style is the ability to be true to yourself and your tastes. There are women who can pull off an outfit that you would never dream of wearing. Stylish women can make something so simple look so damn awesome. That's the secret to doing it well: do it your way, to fit your body type and your style!

## Developing Your Personal Style

This is an opportunity for experimentation and self discovery. Personal style is about developing a sense of self rather than simply following trends, and it will continue to develop as you continue to experiment.

The key to looking great is staying true to your personal style. Style is timeless. Someone who is stylish may or may not follow fashion trends, but they always stay true to their own aesthetic. Just because it is a trend does **not** mean it is good for you, your body type or your style. It is better to be **current** rather than **trendy**.

Choose an overarching style that you feel drawn to, be it classic, minimal, edgy, boho, feminine or preppy. Once you have a general idea of your style you can use that as your starting point. When I style a woman I always ask if she can tell me a little bit about her personal style. So many women do **not** have an answer! This brings me great joy because this is where we can really have some fun: discovering a woman's personal style! For me, this is **game on**!

Don't worry if you are still unsure about your own personal style. It's something that continues to evolve and develop as time goes on, and you become more attuned to it. Personal style is **not** about conforming to fit into one of those categories. Consider some of the most stylish women you know. They all dress in a way that is not so much about fashion, but rather a very personal interpretation of who they are. They are awesome in selecting colors, cuts, fabric, and most importantly the shapes that celebrate their **best** features and spirit.

Finding your personal style isn't something you can do overnight. But there are strategies you can use to learn more about the clothing that works for you! Follow your instinct. Don't be afraid of trying new things or making mistakes. There are times when I look back at an outfit in a post from my boutique and think, what was I thinking? If you get it wrong once in a while, it's no big deal! Personal style comes from within, and it starts with what excites you, what looks amazing on your body type and what you're instinctively drawn to.

## Answer These Questions

Here are some questions to help you begin:
- Which items and silhouettes am I most drawn to?
- What is the color palette of my wardrobe? *Build your signature uniform around this color palette.*
- What is my lifestyle?
- How many uniforms do I need: work, leisure time, dress up, etc? *It's ok to have several uniforms! Different activities or events require different styles.*
- Which is my favorite outfit to wear?
- What do I feel most comfortable wearing?

- What do I have the most of in my wardrobe? *This is a guide towards uniform dressing.*
- Which of my outfits do people compliment the most? *When you feel comfortable in something, people tend to notice your confidence.*

## Developing Your Style Uniform

The most amazing woman in the room has something more powerful than just the right clothes, hairstyle, and makeup: she has confidence . . . it's the single most beautiful thing a woman can wear every day. The best way to achieve this confidence is to develop your unique personal style uniform. Here is how you can do that:

**1 EVALUATE THE CLOTHES YOU WEAR**
Look at your closet. Which items are your favorite? Which items make you happy? Which items receive the most complements? Pull these pieces out and think about why they make you feel good. How do they fit? What do they have in common?

**2 KNOW WHAT YOU LIKE**
When developing your style, it can sometimes be easier to start with what you ***don't*** like, and then rule these out when creating your style uniform.

I don't like bright colors or flowy clothing, so it does not make up part of my wardrobe – ever! When we rule things out, we will naturally become aware of what feels good to wear. Once you have a feel for what works for you, stick with it, no matter what trends or fashion fads may come and go.

## 3  THE ART OF HIGH/LOW DRESSING

The art of mixing casual and dressy gives you more to wear without adding anything new to your wardrobe. It is all about finding that sweet spot where a cotton tee meets a structured blazer, or where jeans are paired with an expensive silk blouse. Your fancy items are not only for special occasions; your blazer is not only for the office; and your sneakers are not only for exercise. Pair a silk tank top with your denim skirt, and add those fabulous sneakers. Wear your favorite suit trousers with a chunky knit sweater and some sneakers. Take your most comfortable jeans, a basic tee and sneakers, and add a high-end designer handbag and belt. One of my new favorites is taking a bias cut skirt, and matching it with a chunky sweater and sneakers. Just have fun and experiment with unlikely duos… they make the best outfits!

## 4 KNOW YOUR BODY

Learn to emphasize your best features and be objective about your body shape. ***Please*** stop focusing on the flaws that you see when you look in the mirror. ***Remember, it's lying to you!*** Everyone has flaws, some are just better at camouflaging them. What are your best features? How can you accentuate them? Discover what shapes, styles and fabrics are the most flattering for your particular silhouette. If you have curves, clothing that drapes and moves in and out with your curves will flatter. Straighter body shapes are enhanced by clothing that falls in a straight line. There is clothing for every body type. Also, don't get hung up on a size or think there is something wrong with you when the clothes don't fit. It's the clothes, not you!

## 5 MIRROR THOSE YOU ADMIRE

When evaluating your style, look to women whose fashion you love. Start with family and friends whose style you admire. Learn about different style types and identify the ones with which you most align. For outfit inspirations, scroll through instagram, pinterest or fashion magazines and find outfits you can replicate with pieces you already own. You might even discover that you already have pieces you love, you just haven't been styling them in ways that fit your body and style.

## 6  CREATE A CAPSULE WARDROBE

Classic, timeless pieces never go out of style and buying them in your most flattering neutrals is one of the best investments you can make in your wardrobe. Create a collection of basics that you can mix and match to create effortless looks. Don't skimp on great pieces such as a classic white shirt, great blazer, fabulous t-shirts, denim jacket, great fitting jeans and those awesome black pants that make your butt look great! Keep the ones that make you feel great and replace everything else with items that really work for you. These items may be simple, but they'll help you show off your unique style by providing a foundation for more exciting pieces. They will easily stand the test of time and can be used year after year with other items in your best accent colors.

## 7  KNOW YOUR COLORS

Find and wear colors that match your natural coloring and are the most flattering for you! If you don't already have a palette of go-to colors that you know make you look amazing, do yourself a favor and find out what your color palette is. It will make shopping and dressing so much easier. It's important to know what colors make you look your best. While some people look great in black and white, others look best in a softer palette, such as navy and cream. Explore to learn what colors express your personal style.

## 8  STEP OUTSIDE YOUR COMFORT ZONE

Personal style is all about playing with fashion to discover which clothes make you look and feel your best. Once you've built your capsule collection, it's time to add unique pieces to your wardrobe that show off your style personality. This might involve some experimentation. Clothes are supposed to be both fun and inspiring! Play around and try new things; there is no right or wrong on what makes *you* feel and look amazing! If you absolutely love something that is outside of what you would normally buy, and it makes you feel awesome, go for it! The key is, be willing to experiment. Start with something small, such as a piece of jewelry, and see how it feels wearing it. **Great** personal style is unique to *you*.

## 9 ACCESSORIZE!

Accessories are a part of your uniform that differentiates your look from everyone else. We are often advised against wearing too much jewelry, but the fact is, most women don't wear enough. Well selected jewelry and accessories are the secret that brings pieces of clothing together and creates a fabulous and stylish outfit! Handbags, earrings, scarves, belts, shoes, and even nail color, all reflect who you are and make your personal style authentically yours. Choose accessories that highlight rather than dominate or overpower you and that allow your beauty to shine! It's the details that make your style uniform uniquely yours.

## 10 ACCEPT YOURSELF EXACTLY AS YOU ARE

I hear it *every* day – women are waiting for the moment they become a certain size and weight. That day may or may not arrive. Learning to be comfortable with your looks and dressing in a way that reflects who you are, are key components for developing your own personal style. Fashion is not about the compliments you'll receive, but the confidence you'll feel. Your style should be a reflection of who you are, ever-evolving and unapologetically you!

## FINDING YOUR STYLE UNIFORM

Having a uniform is the highest level of style. It means a woman is totally confident and is not influenced by outside opinions or trends. As you develop your style uniform, it will help you know how to always look put together. Let's take a look at that in the next chapter.

## STYLE FILES
## Feminine Fashion

*I love helping women look and feel beautiful. It is heartbreaking for me to see women look in the mirror and feel sad and frustrated! That is why I do what I do in my boutique, and why I wrote this book. I have so many stories to share of women who transformed in just a few hours to feeling beautiful, and I want to share a few of these stories with you:*

Let me tell you a style story...

Samantha is a self proclaimed tom-boy and needed help dressing in a more feminine way without wearing bows and flowers. We started with the basics. Feminine styles are the most classic ones. We opted for a timeless look with a skirt and blouse. It was a soft floral of creams and blues. She loved it since she could mix and match both pieces for additional looks. I had her attention!

Next we went for some cute dresses in solid colors that she could dress up with heels or down with a sneaker. Then we added accessories! I knew that less would be more with Sam. We chose a few delicate pieces that complimented her outfits.

We also went over her shoe choices. Heels are a must for dressing more feminine. I have shoes to try in the fitting rooms and I put a nice mid-heel on her to show her what a difference it makes!

Finally, I explained to Sam that the key to dressing more feminine is to embrace it! Wear what makes you feel pretty and confident and forget about what everyone else is wearing! Sam wore one of her outfits right out the door as it made her feel feminine and fabulous!

> **DRESS SHABBILY** AND THEY REMEMBER THE DRESS; **DRESS IMPECCABLY** AND THEY REMEMBER THE WOMAN.
>
> ~ COCO CHANEL

Chapter 2

# Foolproof Ways To Always Look Stylish

Looking put together leaves a lasting impression. And you want that impression to be fabulous! It does **not** take a lot... it's just the small details that can make **all** the difference. Looking put together does not have to cost a lot of money or take a lot of time, and may not even involve clothes – but it does require a little effort every day. Once you start making these steps part of your daily routine – your habit – it will feel like no effort at all – especially because of how amazing you will look!

## To Make a Fabulous Impression:

**1  SKIN AND NAIL CARE**

Your skin is one of the first things that people notice. Well cared for skin looks beautiful bare and creates the perfect base for makeup. Keep your skin moisturized. A tinted moisturizer with SPF keeps the skin hydrated, evens out your skin tone, and prevents sun damage.

Manicured nails are essential for nail health, and not only create a good base for nail polish, but also look beautiful bare. Nails don't need to be painted, provided you take the time to shape and file them. Apply a cuticle cream to keep bare nails moisturized and strong.

**2  USE LIPGLOSS OR LIPSTICK**

Lipgloss and lipstick should be thought of as an accessory; they add color to your look, and brighten your appearance. When you wear a bold lip (like red), keep the rest of your makeup light so it does not compete with your lips. If bright lips are not your thing, try a lightly tinted lip gloss.

## 3 USE MASCARA AND CONCEALER

If you don't have time for a full face of makeup or you are just not that girl, at least take time for some concealer and mascara. Concealer hides dark, under-eye circles and blemishes for flawless looking skin. Mascara makes eyes look fresh and beautiful. Looking in the mirror is a lot more fun when you take a little time to enhance your natural beauty. *You* will feel better and more confident.

## 4 DO YOUR HAIR

Having messy hair is no way to look put together. Always do your hair before you leave the house. Drying and styling your hair in the morning can take a lot of time, so consider skipping the wash and opting for a dry shampoo spray – they really work! Dry shampoo can also add volume and texture to hair so you will never have a bad hair day. If you don't have time to style your hair, try a fun ponytail or classic bun.

## 5   KEEP A PAIR OF SUNGLASSES ON HAND

You can't look put together if you're squinting in the sun whenever you go out, plus it adds wrinkles. Sunglasses will always make you look chic on the go. Want drama? The bigger the better!

## 6   INVEST IN QUALITY PIECES

Investing in a handful of quality pieces (like blazers, shoes, and sweaters) can help you look put together every day with little effort. When shopping for these investment pieces, stick to neutral colors, like black, navy, camel, and gray, as these colors go with anything and they make a good canvas for adding a pop of color.

## 7   PAY ATTENTION TO FIT

The fit can make or break an outfit. Too big is almost as dreadful as too small. The best thing to do to get the right fit is to *ignore the size!* Look in the mirror, use the guidance of a sales associate or the opinion of a good friend – one with great taste – to give you the honest truth.

**8**   **WEAR DARK WASH JEANS**

When given a choice between dark wash and light wash, I always choose dark. Dark wash will always look more polished and is slimming.

**9**   **STYLE YOUR LOOK**

Cuffing your jeans, rolling your sleeves, popping your collar and scrunching up your blazer sleeves are details that can transform a boring outfit into an awesome outfit.

# Fashion Don'ts

Mistakes – we all make them. And while some are weightier than others, it's fair to say that we'd all like to avoid them. Though fashion mistakes may not matter as much as other mistakes in life, they do count, and here's why: they make you *feel* as though you don't look good, which means you won't feel confident – and remember, confidence . . . it's the single most beautiful thing a woman can wear every day! So here are some of the fashion guidelines.

**1 DON'T WEAR TOO MANY TRENDS**

Embracing too many current trends or logos all at the same time can make you look insecure, and as though you feel like you need to fit in or gain the approval of others by wearing what's popular. Not only that, too many trendy pieces and logos take a stylish outfit and turn it into a cluttered and confusing one. Does this mean you should avoid new trends and logos like the plague? Of course not! Just stick to one or two trends or logos at a time to keep your look cohesive.

**2 DON'T WEAR CLOTHES THAT ARE BAGGY**

Though some may say that baggy clothes are stylish, the truth is, baggy clothes are hard to pull off in a flattering way. For most, they come across as frumpy, ill-fitting, or the wrong size. Simply put, oversized clothing can make you appear larger than you are.

**3 DON'T WEAR CLOTHES THAT ARE TIGHT**

Just as wearing clothes that are too baggy can be unflattering, wearing clothes that are too tight is also not attractive. This can make you look uncomfortable, and it can highlight imperfections and insecurities. Instead of tight clothing, opt for clothes that fit well and flatter your figure. Proper fit is important for a polished appearance – we want to enhance your silhouette and body type! Skimming the body is just right. One way to wear fitted clothing is to balance your outfit.

Fitted Top + Wide Leg Pant<br>
Skinny Jean + Looser Tunic Top<br>
Swing Dress + Structured Jacket

## 4 DON'T WEAR TOO MUCH MAKEUP

There's a time and a place for a glam look, but for your day-to-day life, heavy makeup can age you and easily look overdone. Instead of caking it on, opt for a more natural look to enhance your features.

## 5 DON'T IGNORE YOUR PERSONAL STYLE

With all this talk about fashion rules and common fashion mistakes, you may think that your style doesn't matter. Not true! Your overall look is only as good as you feel. Don't wear a certain color if you hate it. Try not to be swayed by trends if they don't align with your personal style. You do not need a wardrobe full of clothes you won't wear or less money in your wallet. It's important to dress in a way that not only reflects your personality and style, but also your lifestyle and budget.

## 6 DON'T CLING TO OUTDATED TRENDS

Since we are talking about trends, wearing outdated trends can make you look and feel out of touch. Yes, it's true that everything comes back around, but it does not mean you need to partake or hold onto everything in the hope that it comes back.

## 7 DON'T LIMIT YOUR STYLE

So, you're stuck in a style rut but you're hesitant to try anything new. If you do not experiment with different styles it can be a fashion mistake because it limits your creativity and self-expression! Fashion is more than just a function, it's a form of art. By sticking to a single style or look, you may miss out on the opportunity to explore new textures, colors, and silhouettes. When you're discovering your personal style, experimenting with different styles allows you to discover what works best for you and helps you develop your own unique style sense.

## 8 DON'T BUY POOR QUALITY FABRIC

Always feel the fabric. It should feel great! Is it too thin? Can you see panty lines? Does it wrinkle terribly when you crunch it? All great questions to ask before you purchase. I no longer view spending money on clothes as frivolous spending. I see it as an investment in myself and in my confidence.

Avoiding these common fashion mistakes is essential for crafting a polished and put-together look. By avoiding pitfalls like frumpy clothing, low-quality pieces, and improper fit, you can elevate your style – and even better, elevate your confidence in your appearance.

## STYLE FILES
## Petite Styling

Let me tell you a style story…

It can be a challenge for petite women to find clothes that fit their body. Shopping for clothes when you're petite can feel like trying to solve a fashion puzzle. My client Shirley told me that sleeves are always too long, and pants need hemming. That is a lot of work. Petite women generally have a smaller frame, meaning garments like long tops or oversized clothes can overwhelm their shape and throw off their proportions.

All she needed was the recipe for dressing her body type. I gave Shirley a *petite class* in styling with these insights:

- high-waisted pants create longer legs
- monochromatic outfits create the appearance of height
- skirts that hit at or above the knee make the legs look longer
- V-necklines lengthen the neck
- pointed shoes add length to the legs
- belts are cinched at the waist
- use delicate jewelry and smaller bags

Using all the tips that I had just taught her we started with the bottoms. We don't carry petite bottoms but a high rise crop was just perfect for her height. No alterations necessary!

I showed her how crop tops or a front tuck make her legs look longer and her look taller. She screamed, "OMG Sher, this stuff really works!" Lucky for petite women, crop tops are a huge fashion statement right now and so easy to find. I taught her the bunny tie, which really makes your legs look longer.

I put her in a couple of outfits that were all one color, top and bottom, with a pointed toe. We were together for almost two hours and she was a new woman. The fear of dressing was gone because no one had ever explained the correct proportions for dressing her petite body type. We did have to have a couple of the pants altered, but that was easy.

Shirley left a ***very*** happy client as she said she will practice each and every one of these tips when she buys in the future.

# FASHIONS FADE, STYLE IS ETERNAL.

~YVES SAINT LAURENT

## Chapter 3

# Clothing That Goes With Everything

Do you ever find yourself staring at your closet, unsure of what to wear? Do you wish you had a go-to outfit that always looks put-together? You're not alone in this frustration. Many of us have experienced the feeling of not knowing what to wear or how to put together a cohesive look. You are about to banish wardrobe frustrations for good. I've worked with thousands of women to build a wardrobe they love. A key component is identifying the wardrobe basics that every woman needs.

Having the basic versatile clothing items in your wardrobe gives you ease and versatility and means you always have something to wear. There is a list of nine essential items that go with everything. These versatile pieces will create a variety of stylish outfits that will make getting dressed a breeze. Let's dive in and discover the clothing items that go with everything to elevate your style, and make getting dressed a whole lot easier:

## A White Tee

Every woman needs a white tee. In fact, I am wearing one right now as I write. The classic white tee is the unsung hero of the fashion world, effortlessly bridging the gap between easy-going casual and understated chic. It's a blank slate for countless outfits.

Picture it under a blazer for an instant touch of sophistication, or paired with your favorite fleece for that cool, model-off-duty look. From mornings when you crave simplicity to evenings that call for a touch of laid-back elegance, the classic white tee is there for you; and it will **never** go out of style. Does a white tee really match everything? Yes! This staple looks as good with jeans and sneakers for a casual day, as it does with heels and a pencil skirt for a night out.

## A Button-Down Shirt

Even if your life doesn't involve business meetings, think about how a button-down can be worn for weekend brunches, shopping days, or family dinners. You can tuck it into the waistband of your go-to jeans for a touch of casual elegance, or pair it with a structured skirt for those moments that call for a bit of polish. It is a great travel piece you can layer over a tank top and leggings for a cute travel outfit. Opt for timeless shades like pristine white or classic stripes. A button-down is the ultimate chameleon, ready to complement every outfit with style.

## Jeans

Matching everything in your closet, jeans have the ability to morph from the foundation of a laid-back ensemble to the base of a chic, polished look. Even better, there's a pair for every body shape, whether you prefer the sleek appeal of slim jeans or the relaxed vibe of boyfriend cuts. Find a pair that celebrates your shape (see Chapter 5). Envision dressing jeans with a sophisticated top and statement heels for an evening out, or keeping it effortlessly cool with a simple tee and your trusty sneakers for weekend adventures. Jeans are the backbone of a wardrobe and they offer both comfort and style, no matter the occasion.

## Black Pants

Black pants are a versatile wardrobe staple ready to tackle any outfit dilemma with ease. They create so many options! They can play the sophisticated counterpart to your classic white tee, creating an outfit that's the perfect balance of casual chic, or they can anchor a more vibrant, patterned top (like a leopard print – my personal fav). Black pants have the ability to straddle the line between formal and casual, making them ideal for a seamless transition from a day at the office to an evening out with friends. There are many different styles: from dressy to structured and tailored, and from high-waisted to wide-leg pull-on pants. Select a fit that flatters your figure so you will want to wear them again and again.

## A Sweater

A well-chosen sweater is a key element in your wardrobe for all seasons. From cashmere to cotton to wool, the fabric and style options are endless and only determined by your lifestyle, climate, and budget. Whether it's the contrast of a chunky cable knit paired with sleek trousers, or a fine lightweight option layered over a dress for transitional weather, the right sweaters can elevate the simplest looks with ease and elegance.

## A Denim Jacket

Offering both warmth and effortless style, this is a go-to for chilly mornings. The right denim jacket is an essential piece that adds a touch of texture, layering, and depth to your outfits. This piece effortlessly layers over anything from a delicate dress to your cherished jeans-and-tee combo, seamlessly blending comfort with your personal style.

## White Sneakers

You may think that white sneakers are too casual to go with everything. Wrong! While they may not suit every occasion, they can go with almost every item in your wardrobe. Thanks to their simplicity, they are a blank canvas that complements every color and texture in your wardrobe. Whether you're pairing them with a flirty dress to bring a sporty edge, slipping them on with your favorite jeans for a casual look, or pairing them with a maxi skirt for a fun mix of styles, white sneakers offer effortless style.

## Black Ankle Boots

Black ankle boots combine versatility with a little bit of edge. They're the secret weapon in your closet, ready to elevate any outfit. Wear them with a breezy dress for a nice contrast, or let them ground your favorite denim for a look that's effortlessly cool. Whether it's a casual daytime look or a night out, black ankle boots have your back. The trick is finding a pair that feels as good as they look. Opt for a comfortable chunky heel and durable material, like leather, so your investment only gets better with time.

## The Blazer

The beauty of a blazer lies in its power to transform any outfit from good to great. It instantly sophisticates a pair of jeans or adds a structured contrast to a flowing dress. A blazer creates an air of confidence for both polished and casual outfits. It seamlessly transitions from boardroom to brunch with ease. It's crisp, clean, and undeniably chic, working seamlessly with everything from weekend denim to a cocktail dress. Whether thrown over your shoulder for a touch of nonchalance or buttoned up for a sleek sophistication, the blazer is your wardrobe's secret weapon. Opt for timeless hues like black, camel, or navy, ensuring it complements your wardrobe.

## How to Wear a Blazer

- Pair it with jeans, a white tee, and sneakers for a casual, chic look, or with jeans and heels for a more polished look that's perfect for dinner dates, casual Fridays, or a weekend brunch. The blazer elevates your denim while the jeans keep things approachable and relaxed.
- For something a bit more elevated, layer your blazer over a slip dress. The structured blazer balances the fluid femininity of the slip without feeling overdone, making it ideal for date nights or even events.
- Want to look seriously sophisticated? Pair your blazer with tailored trousers for a modern take on office dressing. The look requires a bit more attention to proportions. Make sure the silhouettes complement rather than compete – but when done

right, it has a serious wow factor and works beautifully for important meetings or professional events.
- Dress it up for a formal event by wearing it over a dress or pairing it with a pencil skirt.
- For something fun and on-trend, belt an oversized blazer and wear it as a dress. You'll need a longer, roomier blazer to pull this off properly, but it's a playful way to maximize your investment piece. Perfect for brunches, casual parties, or any time you want to look effortlessly chic.
- Timeless, tailored, and totally worth it… a blazer truly is a wardrobe MVP (Most Valued Piece). It instantly elevates any look while maintaining that fresh, classic appeal that never goes out of style. Once you discover how versatile this piece really is, you'll wonder how you ever lived without it.

These nine timeless wardrobe staples are the clothing items that go with everything. These essential pieces not only stand the test of time, but also serve as the backbone for endless style possibilities. The key to a truly great outfit isn't in following the latest trends: it's all about curating a collection of pieces that reflect your personal style, while offering the flexibility to mix and match with ease.

Before you run off thinking that you have to buy all new pieces, take some time looking for these staples in your own closet. Go back over this *basics list*, and then spend time in your own closet doing a thorough search for what you already have. You may be surprised at what you find! And then, follow these style tips:

## Make Old Outfits Feel New

Remember, you don't have to buy a new outfit every time you go out or have an event. Each month I go through my closet to find clothes that I have forgotten about. I can clean out the items that I don't need any longer and take to the women's shelter. The best surprise is finding things that I can mix or match for a completely different look. It is a great game – and fun!

## Add a Pop of Color

Nothing adds zing to an old outfit quite like a pop of color! You can accessorize with bold and bright jewelry, incorporate a bright and playful scarf, pair a bold jacket with neutrals, add a pop of color with shoes or a bag, and experiment with bright patterns. This is one of the easiest ways to make your old outfits feel new. Even your most basic pieces can feel refreshed with a bit of color. The key is to add little bits of color to your basic pieces, making items like jeans and a plain t-shirt seem new.

## Accessorize!

Usually my motto is *less is more* but sometimes, more *is* more – especially when you're looking to refresh your wardrobe. Here's permission to pile on the accessories! I love a bold statement earring, or layer your favorite necklaces together or layer bracelets with your watch to make your own signature look. I **love** the look of a stack of pearls!

A simple white tee does not seem so simple once you've added on lots of accessories. Make this tip work for your own personal style.

## Add a Print

Sometimes the right print can take a cool outfit and make it even cooler. Start with your favorite go-to outfit and add in a print. Prints are very personal, so wait and find ones that you really love! I'm all about a fab leopard print! You **don't** have to constantly wear a new trend or spend a lot of money to have a new style. Most importantly: experiment and have fun!

## STYLE FILES
## Belly Basics

Let me tell you a style story...

Karen came into the Boutique not feeling great about her body, especially her tummy. I told her she came to the right person as it is my specialty.

First, we discussed the basics – choose the right undergarments. The right undergarments and lingerie boost your confidence and also provide ample support to your frame. High rise undergarments tuck in your belly jiggles. Invest in the right shape-wear. It can work wonders by smoothing out any lumps and bumps.

Embrace high-waisted everything! From jeans to skirts, anything that sits above your natural waistline can help create a smoother silhouette. These pieces cinch in your waist and hold in your belly, giving the illusion of a flatter tummy. Karen and I started with a pair of high rise, straight-leg jeans from Spanx. She **loved** them and said she may never take them off!

Karen told me she had a ton of low rise jeans. I told her to take them to the shelter and **only** wear high rise bottoms. Low rise bottoms end below the tummy and further add to stomach bulges, making the muffin top look bigger than it actually is. Even if low rise jeans are in trend, get rid of them. It is better to create your own trend rather than end up a fashion disaster.

The fabrics and cuts you wear determine how your outfit looks more than your body fat does. So for tops, Karen and I chose flowy fabrics. I taught Karen how to do the front tuck and then showed her the bunny tie, which is great for hiding the tummy, too! We opted for dark colors and subtle prints. If you love prints go for smaller patterns that create a more streamlined look.

I brought her a peplum top. A peplum hemline is ideal for all the women who have the muffin top figure. They magically make you look slim while offering you enough room to breathe and stay comfortable.

Karen had sleek, slender, sexy legs so I suggested we style outfits in a way to give attention to her legs. We tried a couple of short skorts with the same tops and tuck – she looked amazing!

Karen was so happy – no one has ever spent this much time teaching her how to dress for her body type. I was so happy for her – but we were **not** finished yet! Wrap dresses are great for hiding belly fat. Not only do they look elegant, classy and feminine, but also a wrap around flap hides your tummy in the most effortless way possible. Plus, you can cinch the dress around your waist to give it a well-defined shape. The *fit and flare* effect of a wrap dress helps you strike the right balance between your upper and lower torso, and adds a slimming effect.

Karen was almost in tears. She left with two large bags of clothes, and even more importantly, the education on how to dress for her body type.

> **THE DRESS MUST FOLLOW THE BODY OF A WOMAN, NOT THE BODY FOLLOWING THE SHAPE OF THE DRESS.**
>
> ~ HUBERT DE GIVENCHY

# Chapter 4

# Slim Secrets

*Yes!* The chapter you have been waiting for. We *all* want to look our best, right? These are some of the tricks I have been using for years – and they work! They will make you look taller, slimmer, longer, and leaner. If you use all of these, you may just disappear!

## Column Dressing

Wearing all one color helps to elongate the body. A uniform, distraction-free outfit results in a taller, slimmer appearance. Opting for monochrome outfits, especially in darker tones like black, navy and brown, is a brilliant strategy. They tend to create an unbroken vertical line, streamlining the body and giving the illusion of slimness. Lighter tones and neutrals, such as a white top paired with white pants or a beige duo, can also be very effective. To keep a monochrome outfit from appearing dull, add texture by mixing different fabrics, or add a pop of color with accessories. A scarf is a great way to add style to a solid-color outfit. Always make sure that you keep the bottoms of the scarf uneven. You do not want to have a straight line across the hip area as it will create the illusion of width.

## Create Cuffs

This is a biggy! **Always** roll your shirt and blazer cuffs for a leaner look. Rolling your cuffs to a 3/4 length will make your hips immediately look slimmer. It differentiates where the hips stop and the arms start. Style tip: If your cuffs won't stay up, use a hair tie band on each sleeve. Start with your sleeve down, put each hair tie over each cuff and then roll the sleeve over the hair tie. Sleeves will stay up and no one will know your secret!

## Pop Your Collar

This is like telling the world, "I put thought into my outfit, but I'm not trying that hard." A popped collar will immediately make you look taller and is quite fashionable! There are two ways to keep your collar popped.

Take an iron and starch your collars or take a bobby pin and slide it top down over the back of the collar. It does not show and will keep your collar perfectly popped! So easy and *no* iron needed.

## Front Tuck

This is easy and effective in making your legs look longer and you leaner. To achieve the front-tuck, you simply tuck the front portion of your top inside the button of your pants, and let the sides fall over the waistband. Let it hang loose in the back. Adjust until you feel it looks right. To ensure it does not come untucked during your day, tuck it in so it is taut and tight. Then extend your arms straight up over your head. It will automatically pull out just enough to make the perfect front tuck.

## Twist and Tuck

This one is a little more complicated but so worth it! Use this whenever your shirt is too long to use the front tuck. Take your t-shirt or blouse and put the fabric in your hands and cinch it up to your waist line like a tail. Twist the tail tight with both hands and tuck it in your bottoms. Let the sides fall over the waistband and let it hang loose in the back. Once you have this mastered you can also use the twist and tuck in the back. Just pull the fabric in the back in the same way you did in the front, twist and tuck in the back of the waistband of your pants. Then just let the front and sides fall over the waistband.

## V-Necks and Long Necklaces

To appear taller and slimmer, outfits with v-necklines can visually lengthen your upper body while elongating your neck. You can pair these with long necklaces, which create the illusion of length and height. Achieving this elongating effect doesn't require a deep plunge. Unfastening just a few buttons on your shirt or opting for a subtle v-neck can work wonders to highlight that vertical line.

## High-Waisted Bottoms

High-waisted bottoms are a fantastic choice when trying to look taller and slimmer. They naturally cinch your waist and elongate your legs. If you are petite, you **must** buy petite, high-waisted bottoms or they will be too high.

Invest in high-rise jeans, skirts, or pants for the instant tall and slim effect.

## Heels and Wedges

One effective yet stylish way to look taller and slimmer is to use heels and wedges. Beyond just adding to your height, the right pair of shoes can elongate the appearance of your lower body. Wearing pointed toe shoes, especially in nude shades, can create the illusion of endless legs. For maximum height illusion, consider a style where the hem of the pants barely skims the floor. This tip adds inches to your legs visually, creating an even longer, more streamlined silhouette.

## Coordinate Shoes and Pants

Here's a simple yet awesome style tip to enhance your silhouette: coordinate the color of your pants with your shoes. This clever trick creates a continuous visual line, making you appear taller and slimmer. It's all about making the eye travel effortlessly through your outfit. This can make a big difference in your style!

## Enhance Your Silhouette

Discovering shape-wear can truly be a game-changer. It offers a quick way to look taller and slimmer by refining your silhouette and smoothing out lines. I use shape-wear especially for events as I just want to create smooth lines in my outfit. It's wonderful how they cinch the waist and visually elongate your figure. Take time to find the right brand that is comfortable to wear and easily smooths under any outfit. Shape-wear can give you a much needed boost in confidence.

Looking taller and slimmer is about smart style choices that play up your strengths. Embrace these easy tips and walk with confidence.

## STYLE FILES
## Bottoms Up

Let me tell you a style story...

One day a woman named Sharon came into my boutique and announced, "It's pretty clear you have nothing to fit me in here!" She was a beautiful size XL, but it was pretty clear that she was not feeling beautiful that day. I introduced myself and told her she was in the right place as I might just surprise her. I *love* a challenge! I took both of Sharon's hands in mine, looked right into her eyes and said, "Will you trust me?" Sharon said she was not sure since she just met me, but she would have an open mind – music to my ears!

I told Sharon, "You are a beautiful woman with amazing eyes and hair." Her answer was, "Well thank you, but I'm fat." I told her she was with the right person as I planned to shock her! First, I had her tell me about her personal style. She loves color, but wears black as it is slimming. She wore all her clothes loose and oversized to look smaller. Since she works from home she does not dress up often, but was open to all my suggestions. That is half the battle!

I told Sharon to completely ignore sizes. It is just a number! Every brand can have a slightly different measurement for what each size is. There is *no* standard. I told her to focus on what fits her body. I told Sharon not to hide behind baggy clothes, but to wear the right size clothes that fit as that is more flattering.

We chatted about undergarments as they create the canvas for clothes, and showed her a selection of Spanx. I explained that every size woman wears them. Undergarments create a foundation for the rest of your outfit. Shape-wear has come a long way, and it is now more comfortable. I wear my Spanx everytime I wear a fitted dress. It makes me feel better in my clothes. Sharon put on one of the boy-short briefs and said she already felt thinner!

We started with a *bottoms up* mentality. Get the bottom right and the rest is easy! We settled on a pair of high-waisted Spanx fitted jeans that elongated her frame and held her tummy in. She felt great in them! Her concern and embarrassment started to turn into, *Oh, I really look good in these and they feel great!*

Now I knew I could start bringing her tops to go with her fab new jeans. They were skinny so I kept all the tops flowy and colorful – **No black** as she had said that was all she ever wore.

We talked a lot about embracing her body and accepting her shape. After 2 hours – yes, 2 hours – Sharon really started to embrace her body. It was like a miracle happening right in front of me! Her confidence returned right there in front of that mirror. She was coming out of the fitting room and modeling for us all! This was **not** the Sharon that had walked into the boutique two hours earlier!

I took her hands again in mine, looked at her and asked how she was feeling. She started crying and said she had never felt more beautiful or confident. Next, I got her a couple of fun dresses and she said she felt like a new woman. (I was so excited – she had me in tears too!)

She bought the jeans and another pair like it in a darker wash. She bought seven tops to mix and match with her new jeans and her new attitude. **And** she said she might never take the Spanx off!

Sharon was ecstatic and said she would never shop anywhere else again! I loved the compliment; but I explained to her that she can shop anywhere now that she knows what looks amazing on her beautiful body! Sharon left with big bags of clothing and an even bigger smile on her face.

> **CLOTHES AREN'T GOING TO CHANGE THE WORLD. THE WOMAN WHO WEARS THEM IS.**
>
> ~ ANNE KLEIN

# Chapter 5

# How To Buy Bottoms For Your Rear End

"Do these pants make my butt look big?" How often have you thought, or even asked that? A woman should look just as good leaving the room as she does entering it! Finding bottoms that fit our butts in that 'just-right way' is a dream come true! No two butts are the same and we are all looking for something fabulous, whether it is to accentuate our curves, lengthen our legs, or lift our rear. Depending on your height and hips you want to find a jean that helps create the right curves to give you the best lift, fit, and figure.

Picture this: you're scrolling through your favorite clothing website or browsing a chic boutique, and you finally stumble upon that jaw-dropping pair of jeans you've been hoping to find. But will they actually fit well, or will they be another fashion failure sitting at the back of your closet? Together, we're going to find jeans that fit just right!

The key to finding those magical jeans begins with a solid understanding of your body type. Are you a curvy queen, a slender sensation, or a petite powerhouse? Be a body detective and find out your body type by focusing on your hips, waist, and shoulders. Here is a run down of body types:

**Hourglass** – your hips and shoulders are balanced, you have a well-defined waist

**Triangle** – your hips are wider than your shoulders, you have a smaller waist

**Oval** – you carry your weight around your midsection, you have a wider waist

**Rectangle** – your shoulders, hips, and waist are about the same width

## BEST Jeans For Hourglass Shapes

- *High-waisted* jeans that sit at your natural waist, highlight your curves, and prevent muffin top.
- *Bootcut or flared* jeans with a slight flare from the knee helps balance out your hips and give you that sleek, elongated look, complementing your curves.

## BEST Jeans For Triangle Shapes

- Aim for creating balance between your hips and shoulders, and emphasizing your narrow waist.
- *Straight leg* jeans are the perfect middle ground between fitted and relaxed, creating a gorgeous proportionate silhouette.
- *Bootcut or flare leg* jeans are thought of by most women as making them look bigger; but instead, it will balance out the proportions in the hip area and create a more even silhouette.
- *High-waisted* jeans with stretch will help accentuate curves.
- *Dark wash* jeans are slimming and make your legs look longer. Pair them with a lighter-colored top to draw attention upward.

## BEST Jeans For Oval Shapes

- Aim for creating the illusion of curvy hips and a defined waist.
- *Mid-rise* jeans sit just below your belly button, offering comfort and a smooth, contoured fit.
- Higher rise jeans help conceal the tummy area.
- *Straight or slightly flared* jeans will elongate your legs and balance your proportions and help draw attention away from the midsection.
- Avoid super-tight or tapered jeans.

## BEST Jeans For Rectangle Shapes

- Aim for adding some curve and dimension to your figure.
- *Low to mid-rise* jeans encourage the waistband to sit slightly lower, giving the illusion of more curves.
- *Jeans with pocket detail* – Embellishments on the back pockets can add some volume and draw attention to your behind.

**If You Are Petite:** choose jeans with a slim fit and shorter inseam to avoid overwhelming you. High-rise jeans can elongate your legs, making you appear taller, but you need to specifically buy a petite size or they will be way too high. Avoid too many embellishments as they can make you look shorter.

**If You Are Tall**: you can wear just about anything! Flared, wide-leg, and cropped will all accentuate your height. Be aware of the rise: low or mid-rise jeans are the best for your body type.

**If You Are Plus-Size:** look for comfort, support and most importantly stretch. (Tip: Make sure the waist has the same stretch as the body.) Jeans with a mid to high rise will look the best and create a great silhouette. Dark wash is always best!

The secret to finding the perfect pair of blue jeans is to try on different styles and brands for your body type and preferences. Choose jeans that look and feel awesome. You want a beautiful shape, but you also want comfort. Always sit in your jeans before you buy them! Remember that denim stretches, so do *not* buy jeans that are too big!

## Pocket Placement

Pocket placement makes a huge difference in appearance. *All* butts are beautiful, but we want to work with what we have to create the best appearance!

**If You Want a Rounded Rear:** try pockets that have flaps, buttons, contrast stitching, beading, embroidery, jewels, or bling on the top half of the pocket. Anything that draws attention to that area helps enhance the illusion of a rounded rear. Pockets that are slightly higher up will also help the butt appear more round.

**If You Want a Flat Rear or a Less Curvy Silhouette:** keep the pockets simple and plain. Larger plain pockets creates a more flat appearance. Pockets that are placed wider apart or lower down will flatten the look of your rear. If you prefer a butt that looks full at the top and flat at the bottom, low pockets are for you.

**If You Want a Full Rear:** add embroidery, bling, or other ornamentation to the bottom half of your pockets. This gives the illusion of fullness and shape to the lower area and pulls attention away from the top. Rounded bottom pockets will also help to round out the lower part of your rear. Keep the bottom of the pocket above where your butt cheeks meet the top of your thighs or even a couple of inches above that so you don't flatten the area instead.

**If You Want a Narrow Rear:** choose pockets that are positioned more closely together, which can help to visually slim your rear view. It draws attention to the center of the butt between the pockets giving the illusion of a narrower butt. Wearing higher-waisted jeans will also give the appearance of a narrow backside. Avoid detailing and embroidery. Choose jeans with mid-size back pockets. You can also create a slimmer butt by choosing darker washes.

**If You Want a Wider Rear:** choose pockets that are set wider apart, add ornamentation and embroidery to draw the eye outward. Lower waisted jeans help give the appearance of more width.

**Bottom Line:** a great way to make a lower-hanging rear end look higher is by choosing a pair of jeans with back pockets that are positioned higher on the seat. This pulls attention upward and away from a saggy bottom. Make sure the bottom of the back pockets never sit lower than the bottom curve of your butt where your cheeks meet your legs, as this will cause the dreaded pancake butt effect.

# Jeans That Fit Perfectly

**COMFORT IS KEY**

No one wants to feel like they're being squeezed to death by their jeans. You want a pair that's comfortable enough to wear all day without constantly adjusting or feeling restricted. Look for jeans with a little bit of stretch in the fabric to ensure maximum comfort. Always sit in your jeans before you purchase to check for comfort and stretch.

There are three kinds of jeans in terms of comfort and stretch, so check for these before buying your next pair:

- ***Super Stretch***: These are made with over 90% cotton, with the rest made with spandex. They're like wearing a cloud! Super comfy but beware – they might lose their shape over time.
- ***Comfort Stretch***: A more balanced blend, usually around a 6:4 ratio of cotton to spandex. They may not feel the comfiest ever, but they'll last long and hold their shape like a champ.
- ***No Stretch***: 100% cotton and a bit tight at first, but wait for it – these jeans will gradually stretch and mold to your body becoming your perfect fit.

## QUALITY MATTERS

Say *no* to saggy jeans! We've all had that one pair of jeans that stretched out and lost their shape after just a few wears – **not** the look we want. To avoid disappointment, be sure to invest in jeans made from high-quality materials. Look for brands with good reviews and a reputation for amazing denim. Trust me, paying a bit more for great jeans will pay off in the long run. Plus, your booty will thank you!

## INSEAM LENGTH – THE SECRET TO LONG LEGS

Inseam length is the measurement from the crotch to the hem of your jeans, and it can make a huge difference in how your jeans fit. If the inseam is too long, jeans can bunch up at the ankle or drag on the floor – too short and you'll be sporting *high waters*. Pay close attention to the inseam length when you're shopping; and don't be afraid to have jeans hemmed if needed.

Long legs? You want an inseam of 32-34 inches. For most women, 30 inches is where it's at, and you can even cuff them if you're feeling extra stylish.

## GO FOR COLOR

The perfect shade of classic blue is always a safe bet, but don't be afraid to experiment with different hues. Dark wash jeans are great for a more dressed-up look, while lighter washes are perfect for casual days. Black jeans are a wardrobe staple and can be dressed up or down effortlessly. Darker color jeans make you look slimmer.

## TRY BEFORE YOU BUY

We know trying on clothes can sometimes feel like a chore. But trust me, it's worth it for the perfect pair of jeans. Different brands and styles fit differently, so don't rely on just your usual size. I'll say it again: always sit down in your jeans to check for comfort.

## DITCH THE DRYER!

Do you want your favorite jeans to last longer? Keep them out of the dryer! Instead, hang them to dry for a perfect fit every time. Dryers cause the heat to mess with that good spandex that maintains the original shape of your jeans.

# The Ins and Outs of Leggings

After a good pair of jeans, leggings are the next staple a woman needs for her lower half. They are one of the most versatile and comfortable wardrobe essentials for women living modern, casual lifestyles. The key is knowing how to wear them in a way that feels chic, flattering, and appropriate. Leggings have come a long way since their streetwear heyday in the '70s and '80s. Today's styles are more sophisticated, structured, and wearable than ever before. Many now mimic the look of jeans (jeggings), with refined fabrics and elevated finishes that make them suitable for everyday wear.

Fabric matters more than you think. If you've ever cringed at the sight of someone wearing sheer, footless tights as leggings, you're not alone. That's not the look we're after. The best leggings for women are thick, opaque, and offer substantial stretch without becoming see-through. Look for:

- Heavyweight ponte knit – structured and polished
- Faux suede-soft and elevated – perfect for fall and winter
- Jeggings (denim leggings) – a great everyday alternative to jeans

- Faux leather – with the right fit, these can be fabulously chic.

Fabrics with a four-way stretch and a high lycra or spandex content will maintain their shape better and offer a more flattering fit. Opt for darker colors like black, navy, or deep charcoal for the most slimming and versatile look.

How should leggings fit? Leggings should hug your body comfortably, not strangle it. If your leggings feel like sausage casings, go up a size. You'll look more put-together and feel a whole lot better. Look for:

- High-rise waistbands that don't roll down
- Wide, flat waistbands that smooth the tummy
- My personal favorites are Spanx *Booty Boost* leggings. I swear my butt goes up an inch every time I wear them!

What are the best tops to wear with leggings? No matter how fit you are, coverage is key. Look for:

- Tunic length sweaters with shape
- Long blazers for a polished finish
- Shirt dresses or long button-front blouses
- Knee-length cardigans layered over a crop top
- Short dresses that feel a tad too short on their own

Look for tops that get to skim your shape. You want length, not bulk. Side slits help with movement and keep the silhouette lean.

Your shoes can make or break your legging outfit. Here are some of the best options:

- Sneakers
- Ballet flats – think Audrey Hepburn (always timeless)
- Ankle booties – perfect for fall and winter, and easy to style.
- Knee-high or riding boots are classic and give an elongating look in cold weather, especially when matched to the color of your leggings.

Don't let anyone tell you that you can't wear leggings! With the right fabric, fit and styling, leggings can be one of the most flattering and functional pieces in your wardrobe. They're comfortable, versatile, and when worn well, classy and stylish.

## STYLE FILES
## Curves

Let me tell you a style story...

I recently had a wonderful experience with a new client named Kamie. She came into the boutique for the first time and went straight to the jeans. I greeted her and asked her how I could just make her day! She said, "You could make my day by taking half my curves!" She said that jeans just don't fit her curvy figure correctly – ever. Well, I love a great challenge and I told her so.

I looked straight in her eyes and asked her to trust me. Lucky for me she said yes! I took her straight to the Spanx jeans as they look great on most figures. Because she has hips I suggested a high waist to show off her fabulous figure, and a flare leg to balance out the hip area. She liked the high waist idea but said that flared legs will just make her look bigger. I asked her to just give it a try. She put on the first and only pair and came out of the fitting room with the biggest smile on her face!

She said, "You are so right!" (They don't call me the Style Doctor for nothing!) No one had ever taken the time to explain how certain styles complement her beautiful curves. She bought the jeans in three different washes and swore she would never shop anywhere else!

These success stories make me so happy.

# EVERY WOMAN MUST HAVE A LITTLE BLACK DRESS.

~ COCO CHANEL

## Chapter 6

# LBD – The Little Black Dress

After its first appearance in American Vogue in the early 1900s, the little black dress (LBD) became more popular. Coco Chanel helped to turn it into a staple that almost every woman had in her wardrobe or closet. I always have at least one LBD in my closet that I look and feel great wearing. This way I am always ready for any event. I would call a LBD the most important thing in your closet!

So, how do you choose the perfect little black dress for you – one that looks like it was made for your body? The perfect LBD makes you feel sexy and beautiful the minute you put it on. It will be your go-to dress, and works for many occasions. Simple silhouettes, like the A-line and sheath, are flattering for most body types.

Know your body. Show off your best features, and hide or disguise your less favorable ones. If your legs are spectacular, show them off with a short, fitted dress. Hemlines that end at the smallest part of your knee will flatter most legs. Here are some suggestions that will work with the various body types – it is all about creating balance. If you are:

- Larger in the middle or on top: a fit and flare or wrap dress
- Straight, no curves: sheath or strapless dress
- Curvy, hourglass, or voluptuous hips and bust: wrap or v-neck dress, especially one that hugs your figure and accentuates your curves
- Larger on the bottom: an A-line dress
- Small waist, defined bust, hips that are wider than shoulders: asymmetrical necklines or off of the shoulder sleeves (helps you appear more proportionate)
- Broad shoulders, narrow waist and hips: longer sleeves and a v-neck
- Defined bust, narrow hips, and petite arms: fuller skirts, low necklines
- Balanced width shoulders, hips, and waist: pleated full skirt, A-line

## Fabric

You will want to wear your LBD year round so buy it in a fabric that can be worn in all seasons. If you spend more time doing casual things, you may lean towards cotton or cotton blends. If you have a dressier lifestyle, perhaps choose silk.

## Color

I know we are talking about the perfect little *black* dress here, but this color doesn't work for everyone. If this is the case for you, choose a neutral color that flatters you: navy, olive green, brown, etc. Find something in your neutral color and use that as your personal LBD. The point is to find a versatile dress that you can wear over and over again and feel fabulous!

When you go shopping, perhaps bring an honest friend (who has great taste) or find a sales associate who you trust. Most of us avoid new shapes or styles, but the perfect LBD might surprise you, so be adventurous and try a variety of options.

## Accessories

Your LBD is like a blank canvas that can be altered for each occasion with accessories, whether it's a wedding, formal event, work, dinner with friends, or a casual shopping day.

**Statement Jewelry** – Most women love an opportunity to showcase their jewelry. A black dress with pearls channels elegance, and is perfect for a wedding. A metallic strappy heel adds a touch of shine. Bold, colorful necklaces, earrings or bangle bracelets can add a pop of color and personality to your outfit. Chandelier earrings are especially transformative.

If you tend to go over the top, remember Coco Chanel's advice: "Before you leave the house, look in the mirror and remove one accessory." I don't know if I believe that, and certainly don't practice it, but I just love to quote her.

**Formal Event** – Gold, silver or rhinestone shoes, jewelry, or purses can provide an elegant contrast against a LBD.

**Scarf** – Choose a brightly colored or patterned scarf. I love this option for evening events since it's often a little chilly, especially if you are sleeveless. You can also wrap a scarf around the handle of your bag for an understated bit of color.

**Handbag** – Depending on the occasion and the dress style, choose a clutch, tote, or crossbody bag that complements the dress. Consider a color, texture, or pattern to add contrast. Silver and gold are always safe bets for evening events.

**Hat** – Depending on the style of the dress a hat can be a chic addition, especially for outdoor events or parties. A great option for casual days is a fedora, baseball cap, or visor with a pair of sandals or sneakers. Sneakers and baseball caps are here to stay – so go for it!

**Belt** – A stylish belt can define your waist and create a flattering silhouette, especially if your dress is more loose-fitting.

**Shoes** – Bright or patterned shoes add a stylish pop to your LBD. Classic black heels, boots, or nude pumps can keep the focus on the dress. Metallics are always a good choice for dressier events.

**Outerwear** – Layer a LBD with a stylish blazer, leather jacket, cardigan, or wrap to change the overall vibe of your outfit.

One of the aspects I love about black in fashion, and the classic little black dress specifically, is its slimming properties. No matter our shape, ladies, we can all look stylish and stunning in black! So, whether you're stepping out for a night on the town or aiming for an everyday chic ensemble, remember that the little black dress isn't just a piece of clothing – it is a statement, a mood, and a symbol of timeless style that's always ready to make you feel like the fabulous, confident woman that you are!

## STYLE FILES
## The Magic Dress

Let me tell you a style story...

One of my clients, Judy, called to tell me she had an emergency! Thank goodness I only live five minutes from the boutique, so I met her there. She needed an LBD for a funeral and only had a sleeveless one, but was going to a cold-weather funeral. She also did not want it to look like a funeral dress as she wanted to wear it again.

It was Judy's lucky day because I just happened to have the magic dress! Why is it magic you may ask? Well, it hides the tummy area well, and can be worn in three different lengths. It is ruched on the sides so it can be adjusted to cocktail, knee, or funeral length. It also has three quarter length sleeves. Even better, it does not wrinkle so is great for travel. It magically fits almost any occasion.

Judy didn't even come out of the fitting room with it on: she was dressed, had it in her hands and said I had saved her life! She then bought it in another color and bought the sleeveless one too! Another day in the happy life of being the *Style Doctor*, helping women look and feel beautiful. I just love my job.

> **GIVE THE GIRL THE RIGHT KIND OF SHOES AND SHE CAN RULE THE WORLD.**
>
> ~ MARILYN MONROE

Chapter 7

# The Shoes that Go with Everything

Yes, Everything!

Every woman needs those staple items in her wardrobe – things that can be worn over and over again, and will never go out of style. Whether you're rushing out the door, or simply don't know what to wear, you know you can always rely on these staple items to look great with everything. When it comes to footwear, you may be wondering, *What shoes go with everything*? Well, the answer may surprise you: a white sneaker!

Here's why: white sneakers are the ultimate fashion chameleons. They blend in with everything! Whether you're dressing up for a night out or keeping it casual for a weekend brunch, these shoes have it all. Plus, white sneakers have this magical way of making you look effortlessly cool, giving you that off-duty look. They can dress down a formal outfit, giving that right amount of *I look great without trying too hard* vibe.

There are countless ways you can style white sneakers with all your outfits. Here are some of the ways:

**Athleisure** – Do you live in leggings? Is athleisure in your DNA? Then this is the look for you! For a comfy yet stylish look, start with some classic white sneakers, of course. Pair them with your go-to legging for that sleek, sporty vibe. Toss on a trendy anorak jacket to finish the look. A sling bag or fanny pack thrown over your shoulders adds a casual touch. Top it all off with a baseball cap for that effortless, just-threw-this-on feel. This is a stylish, casual outfit that does not sacrifice comfort.

**Everyday Wear** – White sneakers look fantastic with jeans, too. Build your outfit around classic white jeans. Add a comfy, neutral t-shirt, and throw on a classic denim jacket. Pop on some hoop earrings and add a stylish tote for a touch of flair. The sleek tote bag and hoop earrings sophisticate your look, while sneakers and denim jacket help keep it casual. The white sneakers tie the whole outfit together – perfect for running errands or grabbing coffee with friends. Want to elevate your everyday casual outfit? Replace your denim jacket with a blazer. The timeless blazer adds class to your look, while the tee and sneakers bring more casual elements, creating an effortlessly chic look.

**Classic Chic** – To add a bit of French flair, try wearing your classic white sneaker with a blazer. Blazers are a go-to in French style. French girls love to pair a formal item like a blazer with a casual item like sneakers. Slip into a crisp, white shirt or t-shirt to match with your blazer for that polished yet relaxed look that's timeless and chic. Opt for your favorite jeans. Toss in a casual tote bag to keep it functional, or practice your high/low and add your fabulous designer bag. The white sneakers tie it all together, adding a fresh and sporty touch – perfect for running errands, grabbing brunch, or even a casual Friday at work – effortlessly chic and comfy.

**Dress It Up** – Nothing screams chic more than a simple black dress and sneakers! This classic look will make you feel stylish and confident. This is a signature grab-and-go outfit for days when you don't know what to wear. Just slip on your dress, throw on that denim jacket or trench, and add your pearl studs and bracelet for some classic flair. The white sneaker keeps you comfy and adds a sporty edge. This is actually my signature style, and I want to share more with you about how you, too, can use this amazing combo.

## Wearing Sneakers with a Dress

Picture a woman with a genuine love for dresses, a passion for fashion, and an undeniable appreciation for comfort. That woman is me; and if you ever spot me strolling down the street, chances are you will see me rocking a dress paired with sneakers. Yes, you heard that right. I am a self-proclaimed *sneakers with dress* enthusiast. I wore 3-4 inch heels to work every day and my feet just don't want to do it any more!

I am excited to share my years of experience and expertise in styling sneakers with dresses. I have embraced this combination wholeheartedly, and it has become my signature style – my way of expressing both my love for fashion and my commitment to practicality. More than just a style statement, this combination is about embracing comfort without compromising on style. It's about celebrating your individuality and expressing your personal flair in a way that makes you feel empowered and confident!

Let's delve into how to pair sneakers with dresses, exploring the possibilities and creative avenues that this fusion offers. Whether you're a fellow sneaker enthusiast or just dipping your toes into this trend, this guide will equip you with the confidence and the know-how to rock the combination effortlessly.

**1 CHOOSE THE PERFECT DRESS STYLE**

The key to a successful sneaker-dress pairing lies in finding the right dress style and silhouette. Opt for flowy maxi dresses for a bohemian and relaxed vibe, or go for flirty mini dresses to add a playful touch. Experiment with different lengths and cuts to discover what suits your body type and personal style best.

**2 ACCESSORIZE WITH FLAIR**

Accessorizing can take your sneaker-dress combination from ordinary to extraordinary. Experiment with statement necklaces, trendy belts, or gold earrings to personalize your outfit and make it truly unique.

**3 EMBRACE COLOR COORDINATION**

Coordinate the colors of your dress and sneakers to create a cohesive and visually appealing outfit. Choose sneakers that match or complement the dominant color in your dress. For a bold statement, experiment with contrasting colors to create eye-catching combinations that make a fashion-forward impact.

**4  PLAY WITH PATTERNS**

Don't shy away from pattern mixing when styling sneakers with a dress. Stripes, florals, polka dots, or even animal prints can add an element of fun and creativity to your outfit. The key is to balance the patterns, keeping one as the focal point and the other more subtle.

**5  LAYER FOR DEPTH**

Layering can elevate your sneaker-dress outfit to new heights. Add a denim jacket, a lightweight cardigan, or a cropped blazer to add depth and texture to your look. Not only does layering provide extra style points, but it also allows for versatility in adjusting to different temperatures and occasions.

**6  CONSIDER DRESS LENGTH**

Pay attention to the length of your dress when styling it with sneakers. Shorter dresses such as mini or above-the-knee lengths create a youthful and casual aesthetic. Mini or maxi dresses add elegance and sophistication to the outfit. Choose the length that suits the occasion and that reflects your personal style.

### 7 CONFIDENCE IS KEY

The most important tip of all is to wear your sneaker-dress outfit with confidence. Embrace the combination wholeheartedly, and let your individuality shine through. Remember that fashion is a form of self-expression. And rocking the trend is a statement of your personal style and comfort.

### 8 EXPERIMENT AND HAVE FUN

The beauty of styling sneakers with dresses lies in its versatility and endless possibilities. Don't be afraid to try new combinations, mix different elements, and step outside your comfort zone. Fashion is meant to be fun and expressive, so let your creativity run wild and enjoy the process of discovering unique and head-turning looks.

# How to Shop for the Best White Sneaker

Have I convinced you yet that white sneakers are a must-have? Are you wondering what the best sneakers are? When it comes to shopping for your white sneakers, you don't just want any sneakers. You want a great pair of high-quality sneakers, because staples like this are meant to last. The good news about white sneakers is that since they're such a staple, you'll find them at just about every retailer, but the bad news is that with all these options, it can be overwhelming to find the best white sneakers for you. I have tried a *lot* of sneakers over the years – here are a few things to keep in mind that will help you find your next personal favorite:

**1 KEEP IT SIMPLE**

In order to make it a truly versatile shoe that you will wear a lot, find a pair with little to no detail on it. A lot of options out there have some kind of detailing, whether it is colored stitching, a scuffed look, or printed designs. If this is your first pair of sneakers, find a pair that is plain white with a simple look. Then add to your collection all you want!

## 2 AVOID DISTRACTING LOGOS

If you stay up to date on what's popular, you may know about the Golden Goose sneakers. These purposefully dirty, white sneakers are on the feet of every fashion influencer with a love for athleisure looks and casual shoes. Beware of the price tag! Adidas is also in the spotlight in a big way. While these brands are bold, there are some that are more subtle. Try to find a sneaker without a logo, or with a discrete and neutral logo.

## 3 COMFORT MATTERS

You don't have to sacrifice fashion for comfort! These will be shoes you reach for again and again, so you want to enjoy wearing them. Wherever you are and whatever you're doing, you're going to have a better time in comfy shoes, so this isn't a place to skimp.

Now you have everything you need to know about wearing that classic white sneaker more of the time. If you are new to this whole concept, try it out and have some fun!

> **WHY CHANGE? EVERYONE HAS THEIR OWN STYLE. WHEN YOU FIND IT YOU SHOULD STICK TO IT.**
>
> ~ AUDREY HEPBURN

Chapter 8

# How to Take the Best Photos Ever

"Smile pretty and say cheese!"

***Ugh***! ***Oh no!*** It's that uncomfortable moment when someone wants to take your picture. Some people are naturals in front of the camera, but most of us are ***not***. We all want to look our best in photos. However, photos tend to make you look larger than you actually are. This can cause you to avoid having your picture taken. A great photo depends on many factors including: lighting, make-up, hair and how you pose your body. There are things you should do and some things you shouldn't. Here are some tips and tricks to make every picture of you look fabulous!

If it is planned, wear a fabulous outfit. If you know photos will be taken, dress for the event. Heels always help with posing and posture. **Wear a single color.** This is one of my slim secrets. Add to that a pair of nude heels and your legs will automatically look slimmer and longer.

# Guidelines for Fabulous Photographs

**1. Be away from the camera.** The person nearest to the camera will always look the largest.

**2. Stay away from skinny people.** I'm *not* kidding! If you must, stand behind them.

**3. Be aware of the sun.** If you are outside, you should stand or sit fully in the sun or fully in the shade.

**4. Pose Sideways.** Keep the *three-quarter* rule in mind. Turning to the side with one foot in front of the other. Your toe should be pointing towards the camera with all your weight on your back foot. This will make you look thinner. Angles and curves make a photo much more interesting and slimming. Always angle your body or face. This will make your shape look more flattering.

**5. Shoulders back, tummy in.** Stand up tall, pull your shoulders back, raise your chest and suck in your stomach. Standing tall comes off as confidence. Practice this in front of the mirror.

**6. Chin up.** No one looks good with a double chin. Stretch your neck slightly and push your face forward a bit. Place your tongue at the roof of your mouth and smile. Tilt your head ever so slightly. Practice this in front of a mirror to find what works best for you.

**7. Create arm space.** A little space between your arms and your body will make them appear thinner. When arms are pressed against your body, they can flatten and appear larger. This is why many female celebrities place their hand on their hips when they pose. Try putting your hand on your hip to create a 90 degree angle. Space between your legs is also important. If you are standing make sure to bend one of your knees just a bit to look natural.

**8. Work your legs.** Try the *walking pose*. Put one foot in front of the other as if you were going to take a step – or keep your legs straight, and turn your right knee inward, while pushing your right toe away from your other foot, keeping it slightly off the ground.

**9. Cross your legs when seated.** Standing will make you appear slimmer. However, if this is not an option, cross your legs at the ankle in front of you. This will make your thighs look slimmer.

**10. Avoid cutting off your limbs.** A common mistake when having your photo taken is to accidentally make it look as if your limbs have disappeared.

**11. Fake it.** If you look and act confident, everyone will think you are a pro and will never know if you feel uncomfortable.

**12. Be natural.** Or at least try! The more comfortable and confident you look, the better the photo. You can have a great picture if you just relax.

**13. Alter your pose.** If multiple photos will be taken, move around for each shot. This gives you a variety to choose from.

**14. Shoot from above.** The best angle for a photo is from slightly above, which will elongate your torso and give you a slim appearance. Run away if the photographer gets on his knees to take the photo! This is the worst position.

**15. Be patient.** It can be uncomfortable to hold a pose while everyone else is getting ready. Just take a nice deep breath and hold that smile!

**16. Be a confident you – look amazing!** Confidence makes for the *best* photos! Practicing at home in front of a mirror is a great idea and will get you comfortable in front of the camera.

**17. Remember – smile!**

# I LIKE MY MONEY WHERE I CAN SEE IT... HANGING IN MY CLOSET.

~ CARRIE BRADSHAW

Chapter 9

# Closet Clean Out

One of the best ways to always look fabulous is to have a closet filled with items you love wearing! This requires regular decluttering, especially as you learn what looks best on you as you purchase new items. You may have some items you loved wearing, but no longer fit your style. They need to go! Decluttering your closet makes getting dressed effortless. Here is how to create your dream closet:

**BE IN THE RIGHT FRAME OF MIND.**

In order to clean out your clothes, you'll need to be ready to LET THINGS GO! Make sure you are rested, fed, and have a good chunk of time to work on your closet. A glass of wine or two may be necessary. Set a limit for the number of items, or hangers, in your closet. Decide on a certain number of items in each category of clothing. For example, maybe you'll aim to keep 15 t-shirts, 10 pairs of pants, 10 work-out outfits, etc. The number will be specific to you, your lifestyle, your preferences and your laundry routine. But the key is to give yourself a limit and to stick to it!

## KEEP TRACK OF WHAT YOU ARE NOT WEARING.

Another way to declutter your closet is to track what items you never or rarely wear. An easy way to do this is to turn all the hangers in your closet around to hang backwards. When you wear an item, hang it back up the right way. At the end of the season, or after a set amount of time, purge any clothes still hanging backwards.

Make a point to wear every item in your closet before wearing something you've already worn. This is a great way to test how much you love each item you're keeping. Try separating your closet in half: one side for clothes you haven't worn yet, and the other side for clothes you've worn. After wearing something from the unworn side, return it to the worn side. If you come across anything you don't want to wear, or didn't look or feel good while wearing, get rid of it!

## USE A MAYBE BOX.

A *maybe box* is one of my favorite tools to help you act more ruthless. It's like a decluttering safety net! Put any items of clothing you're not sure about in a *maybe box*. Seal it, and put it somewhere out of sight. Set a reminder on your calendar for 1-3 months in the future. When the reminder comes up, and you haven't needed, wanted, or even thought about the items in the box at that time, get rid of them. Living with fewer clothes shows you how great a smaller wardrobe can be!

## GATHER ALL YOUR CLOTHES IN ONE PLACE.

I stacked it **all** on my bed! It can be quite eye-opening and even shocking to see all of your clothing in one place. My bed looked like a clothing hay-stack! Pull out anything you don't love, don't wear, or are ready to toss. Bag those items up to be donated.

Next, pull out any clothes that you love, wear often, and are your favorites. Those go back in your closet. Finally, deal with everything that is left. These are the things you neither love nor hate. Try on each item. Only keep items that look and feel good to you. (Here is where you may need that wine!) Each item has to earn its way back into your closet.

## TRUST YOUR GUT.

Pay attention to your first, immediate reaction to each item. Do not keep things out of guilt, money spent, or feeling like you *should* like it. Trust your first reaction to each item. If you don't immediately love it, it needs to go! *Imagine wearing each item and running into someone you want to impress or someone you are meeting for the first time.* This will show you if an item of clothing is worth keeping.

**Use these *tests* and *questions* to be more ruthless when decluttering your closet:**

**1. Does it fit you well today?** If you're expecting your size or shape to change, keep only your absolute favorite items in different sizes. Store them away from your current wardrobe. Not only will you reduce visual clutter in your closet, but also you will get dressed more easily.

**2. Is it in good shape?** Get rid of anything damaged or stained beyond repair, as well as anything that's lost its shape or stretch.

**3. Do you feel great in the item?** Everything in your closet should feel great when you wear it. Get rid of things that you don't look or feel your best in when wearing them, rather than putting them back in your closet.

**4. Do you look great in the item?** Everything in your wardrobe should make you look and feel great when you wear it.

**5. When was the last time you wore the item?** If it's been more than 6 months or even a year, get rid of it!

**6. Does the item work with your current lifestyle?** If you used to work in a corporate setting, but are now retired or a stay-at-home parent, you can get rid of those clothes you no longer need.

**7. Did you buy it but have not worn it?** If you have not been excited to wear a new item after 1 or 2 months from buying it, get rid of it. It can be hard to get rid of never worn clothes, but don't keep things in your wardrobe you're not wearing. Accept it and use it as a lesson to shop more thoughtfully moving forward.

**8. Donate clothes you're removing from your wardrobe!** Bag up those clothes immediately! Don't give yourself a chance to second guess your decisions. If I wait too long I tend to change my mind. We have a homeless shelter here in Naples, and I also take clothes to the two human-trafficking homes here in Naples. It makes the heart feel great, and these women and girls are *very* grateful just to have clothes on their backs.

These tips will help make it easier to simplify your wardrobe and you will ***love*** your new lean, streamlined closet!

## STYLE FILES
# Closet Clean Out

Let me tell you a style story...

I had a client named Marsha. She came to the store and immediately told me she needs nothing as she has a closet full of clothes! I asked her if she wears them all. She responded with, "I only wear a quarter of what is in there!"

I told her to go home, take out all clothing that is torn, stained or faded... easy! Take out anything too small or too large. Next, take out *everything* that does not make you feel fabulous! I wrote it down for her; and she went home with her list and my phone number in hand.

I received a call three days later from Marsha who said she was coming in to shop! I met her at the boutique and asked her about her experience. She said it was awesome and easy as she had her "marching orders from Sher!" She was happy to report that she took eight bags of clothes to the shelter! And now she has plenty of room in her closet to shop. She was so excited!

I got her in the fitting room and we went for it. We had a blast. I brought her ***all*** of my favorite things to start building her wardrobe and her new style uniform. Marcia left with three big bags of clothes that she couldn't wait to wear. And she gave her list to two other friends who eventually came in to shop with me. I now have three new, **very** happy and well-dressed clients!

# GOOD CLOTHES ARE A PASSPORT TO HAPPINESS.

~ YVES SAINT LAURENT

# Chapter 10
# Packing Tips and Tricks

I was your chronic overpacker – the girl who took two suitcases for a weekend and never wore most of what I packed. But I learned that efficient packing saves time, stress, and also allows for more freedom during travel. Here are the steps you can use to pack with ease:

**STEP 1: PLAN**

Get an index card (you could also do this on your phone) and list each of the days you will be away across the top. Then under each day write what the day will be like: include any activities you might do (travel, dinner, dancing, beach, meeting, hiking). This gives you a visual of the trip and the clothes that you will need each day. Once you go through the rest of the steps, you can write in what you plan to wear each day. This may change, but at least it will guide you in order to have enough items, but not too many.

## STEP 2: CONSIDER THE LOCATION

What is the weather? What level of dress will I need? Once you have done a weather check, and know the level of formality you need, then you can begin choosing your clothing. Choose versatile clothing items that can be mixed and matched.

## STEP 3: CHOOSE A COLOR SCHEME

Decide on a color scheme to ensure you can get maximum mixing and matching. I usually choose black and white with a pop of color.

## STEP 4: MIX AND MATCH

Lay *all* of the possibilities out on your bed by group: tops, bottoms, shoes, dresses, etc.

Put outfits together for each day or for each activity (refer back to the index card). This will help you eliminate some items and confirm others. Make sure that each outfit has the accessories it needs (jewelry, shoes, purse). I usually travel in a light-weight sneaker, and take both a dressy heel and a dressy flat or sandal.

- You might take a photo of all your outfits laid out so that you can refer to it while traveling, or in the future when traveling again.
- Try to choose wrinkle-free clothing. Rolling clothes or using packing cubes also helps keep clothes wrinkle free. As soon as you arrive at the hotel, hang up all your clothes. Take any that are wrinkled into the bathroom and turn the shower on to **hot**, close the doors for about five minutes and steam out those wrinkles. **Presto**! Wrinkle free!
- Try using comfy leggings and tank tops or a t-shirt to sleep in. These are more versatile than pajamas.
- Choose a sweater, blazer, or jacket that can go with most of your outfits, or maybe two if your trip is longer.
- Make sure to lay out the extra items like pajamas, workout clothes, socks, underwear, that we tend to forget.
- Choose cosmetics that are all travel size unless you will be gone for too long. Place liquids in a ziplock bag in case they leak. The ziplock also makes security quick if you are not checking a bag.

## STEP 5: CARRY-ON OR CHECKED BAG?

Once you have it all laid out, then you can choose the bag you will need. Can you fit it all in a carry-on or do you need a larger, checked bag? The weight of your checked bag matters. Usually it must be under 50 lbs, but sometimes it is 40 lbs. Carry-on bags are usually included in the cost of your flight, but you still need to keep them under a certain size.

## STEP 6: PACK

Put shoes in first. Use the empty spaces within your shoes to pack smaller items like socks. Then roll each item and place on or in between the shoes to make a flat layer. Then keep adding layers or rolled items. I like to keep item types grouped together for ease of finding them later if I have to search in the suitcase before unpacking. Packing cubes are fabulous and keep everything organized. Add some dryer sheets to keep your clothes fresh and clean during your travels.

Make sure to weigh any checked bags. You can buy a great handheld, travel luggage scale for about $20 to keep with you when you travel so you are never surprised at the airport.

## STEP 7: ASSESS

While you are on the trip, make some notes (on your index card or in your phone) of the items that worked really well, any that did not, and anything you forgot. This way, the next time you travel you have a helpful record of what works for you. We think we will remember, but we do not. You might even print it out and keep it in your suitcase.

For those who travel often, you might have a few travel clothing items that just stay in your suitcase to make it easier to travel. You might also create a checklist on your phone for travel to each of the locations you go to: pool/beach packing list, sightseeing packing list, professional/work packing list, etc.

# IT IS IMPOSSIBLE TO BE STYLISH WITHOUT CONFIDENCE...

~ JANE BIRKIN

# Chapter 11

# The Habits of an Attractive Woman

Deep down we all want to be attractive; but appearance is only a part of what makes us so. Positive attributes and habits contribute to the attractiveness of a woman: how she moves, how she expresses herself, the choices she makes, and how others feel in her company, all help to create a truly beautiful woman. Let's explore the beautiful puzzle of what an attractive women does.

**SHE IS WELL-EDUCATED IN FASHION**

To be attractive, a woman must be well-educated in fashion. This does not mean she needs to spend a fortune on designer clothes, but rather that she has a good understanding of what styles look good on her body, what colors flatter her, and how to accessorize an outfit to make it more flattering. When you understand your body and the basics of fashion, you can dress and style yourself well. (Style tip: If you are still a work in progress to know how to create great outfits, take pictures of yourself when you are shopping and working with an expert so you don't forget!)

## SHE IS ALWAYS LEARNING

Women who are learning new things have a freshness and excitement about them. They keep up with the latest trends and news so that they can be interesting conversationalists. They read books and magazines to learn new things and expand their horizons. They learn from experiences, too, and do not live in regret. The past is the past and it's important to learn from it, but not dwell on it. Most importantly, they know that learning is a lifelong process and they are never too old to learn something new.

## SHE HAS DEVELOPED A SIGNATURE STYLE

Attractive women have developed their own signature style that makes them memorable. Some women are born with a great sense of style, while most have to work hard to find what looks great on them. It's important to try different things until you find something that you're comfortable with and that makes you feel confident. Once you find your signature style, stick with it, and don't be afraid to be uniquely and unapologetically *you!*

## SHE DRESSES FOR HERSELF, NOT OTHERS

Confidence is the most attractive attribute; and a woman who dresses for herself, not for others, is confident and comfortable. When you dress in a way that feels right for your body and personality, it shows.

## SHE EXPRESSES HERSELF IN WHAT SHE WEARS

Attractive women know how to express their individuality through their clothes, hair, makeup, and accessories. Whether it's wearing bright lipstick or having big jewelry, attractive women do whatever makes them feel great about themselves. This makes you unique and memorable. Experiment with different looks, styles, and colors to see what works best for you. You might be surprised at just how good you look when you let your true personality shine through.

## SHE DOES HER HAIR AND MAKE-UP

One of the key components of being attractive is taking care of your appearance. This means making sure your hair and makeup are always done. It makes a huge difference in your appearance, and people notice and appreciate the time and effort you have made. I don't even go to the mailbox without lipstick and mascara!

## SHE HAS A SIGNATURE SCENT

Fragrance is a unique and personal choice based on your preference and on your body chemistry. Having a signature scent helps you feel like yourself, which leads to confidence, which we know makes you more attractive. Fragrance can make a big impression – so experiment and find yours. Many women have a scent for each season, which keeps it fun and fresh.

## SHE TAKES SELF-CARE SERIOUSLY

To look and feel your best, you need to take care of yourself: physically, spiritually, emotionally, and mentally. This means eating well, exercising regularly, having massages, facials, or other healing services. ***All*** of these things work together to help you look attractive and confident from the inside out. You'll have more energy and a general sense of well-being. We women tend to take care of everyone but ourselves, and this makes us angry and bitter. Sound familiar? I am trying to learn how to relax, read books, and of course, write!

If you aren't taking care of yourself, start now. Start by making small changes like adding healthy foods into your diet, or going for a walk every day. Gradually increase the intensity of your workout until you've found a routine that works best for you.

## SHE HAS A GREAT RELATIONSHIP WITH HERSELF

One of the most important habits of attractive women is that they have a strong relationship with themselves. They know and accept their own strengths and weaknesses. They know their own likes and dislikes: what makes them happy, and what stresses them out. They focus on becoming the best version of themselves. Most importantly, they enjoy their own company and do things they love by themselves. Practice loving yourself: take a few minutes to look in the mirror and appreciate all the things you like about yourself. You might be surprised at how truly awesome you really are!

## SHE GETS ENOUGH SLEEP AND RELAXES

A well-rested body will look better than one that is tired or stressed out! Sleeping well helps your body function properly, which means better health. Try going to bed earlier and waking up later in the morning or taking naps. You will be surprised how much better you'll feel once this is done consistently over time. We live in a world characterized by stress. Attractive women know when to take a break from work, both on the job as well as from daily household duties.

**SHE MAINTAINS GOOD RELATIONSHIPS**

Relationships are the sweet spot of life! We are wired for connection. Attractive women understand the importance of nurturing their relationships. They know that these connections bring joy, support, and fulfillment. They also end relationships that are not healthy or supportive. Conflict is part of a healthy relationship; it is inevitable. However, relationships should be peaceful most of the time.

**SHE DOES NOT COMPARE HERSELF TO OTHERS**

Comparison is natural. We compare our looks, our careers, and our relationships to those of others. We can always find someone who seems better than us, and we can always find someone who seems worse than us. But what good does that do? Competition is not attractive. No one can be you and you cannot be anyone else either. The world needs you as you are. Plus, as I say quite often, ***Confidence . . . it's the single most beautiful thing*** *a woman can wear every day.* It makes you freaking attractive. Attractive women focus on their own progress and accomplishments.

## SHE HAS PURPOSE AND PASSION

Having a mission or purpose in life is one of the most attractive qualities a person can possess. Purpose goes hand in hand with passion. Attractive women exude a sense of passion that extends into every facet of their lives. This passion is manifested not only in their personal relationships, but also in their professional pursuits. They channel their enthusiasm into everything they do. Purpose and passion make them attractive and also very inspiring.

## SHE PRACTICES GRATITUDE

Attractive women know it feels good to be grateful. They practice gratitude, even for the small things like a sunny day or going out with a friend. When you are grateful, you see everything as beautiful and meaningful. So next time something goes wrong, stop and find something that makes you feel grateful. It will help you feel more positive and calm, which in turn will make you more confident and attractive!

## SHE SMILES AND LAUGHS OFTEN

Smiling makes you feel happy, and laughter is the best medicine. It's a natural way to boost your mood and feel awesome. Plus, when you smile or laugh, others are more likely to do the same. Attractive women are also able to laugh at themselves, and do not take things too seriously. This makes you more approachable. So if you want to be more attractive, start smiling and laughing more. And who knows? You might even make some new friends along the way!

## SHE POSSESSES CERTAIN ATTRIBUTES

Attractive women possess certain stand-out habits that contribute to their overall appeal. They are: loyal, compassionate, kind, patient, humble, honest, authentic, confident, and on time.

*Loyalty* is the center of a person who values her relationships and treats them with the love, respect, and attention they deserve. A loyal woman stands by loved ones through thick and thin, supporting them during their lows, and celebrating with them at their highs. This loyal commitment makes you even more beautiful!

*Compassion* means putting yourself in other people's shoes.

*Kindness* makes others feel happy and appreciated. There is a joy that fills your heart when you do something for others. It could be as simple as holding the door for someone, being generous with your smile, buying someone lunch, or giving away things you do not need. Attractive women aren't kind to only people they know, they are kind to **everyone!**

*Patience* means waiting for things calmly, without anxiety. Good things come to those who wait. This gives them the advantage of relaxing more and worrying less.

*Humility* is knowing that you are not perfect and can always learn and improve. Humble women are confident without arrogance. Humble women are also good listeners who don't feel the need to be the center of attention. One of my favorite quotes is: *Make tripping part of your dance.* That is humility.

*Honesty* builds safety and trust, and requires confidence. It is attractive when people know they can rely on you!

*Authenticity* comes from contentment with who you are, knowing that whatever others think of you is not important (you do not really have control over that anyway). Attractive women love being themselves and do not seek validation from others.

*Confidence* is key to attracting others. People are naturally drawn to those who know who they are and live as themselves. If you are not that confident, fake it till you make it. The more confident you act, the more confident you will become.

*Punctuality* is one of the most attractive qualities a woman can possess. It shows that she respects other people's time and is capable of planning and organizing her own life. I am *always* early! When you are on time, it relieves stress and helps you feel more in control. Women who are always on time are also generally more organized and efficient, two highly attractive qualities.

So how do you develop all of these habits and qualities? Perhaps focus on a few at a time, and as you master them, move on to the others. Life gives you opportunities if you take them. The attractive women I know did not become attractive accidentally. They became attractive because stuff went wrong and they handled it. They handled it in a thousand different ways on a thousand different days. But they handled it. Those women are my superheroes!

## STYLE FILES

A woman walked up to me at the cafe here in Naples yesterday. She was so sweet and said she had seen me a couple of times and I always looked so "put together." I thanked her as it is so special to me when a woman compliments another woman! I told her I was in the fashion business and had my own boutique here in Naples. We chatted for a bit and then I invited her to come in for a "Fashion Session with Sher."

She said, "How about right now?" So we went to the boutique and she asked me how I know how to dress so well. I thought about it for a second and then told her it just comes naturally to me. She wanted to know what to do if it does not come naturally and I answered with, "Read my book!" I also said, "It is just as much a state of mind as it is the clothing you choose."

My team clapped every time she came out as the outfits were amazing. Her entire attitude about dressing changed along with her confidence! We cried. It was awesome. After two hours in the fitting room we nailed it! We found her the best fashion for her and her lifestyle.

> **IN ORDER TO BE IRREPLACEABLE ONE MUST ALWAYS BE DIFFERENT.**
>
> ~ COCO CHANEL

# Chapter 12

# Stop Wearing These Three Things

This entire book is tips and tricks on how to look and feel your best. Now if I may, I'd like to suggest three things you should *stop* wearing – no matter your age. Don't worry... I'm not coming after your jeans, leggings or comfort clothes. I'm talking about things you wear on the inside. That's where the heavy stuff usually lies. It may not come naturally, and will require some practice, but it will get easier to remove these things forever from your life.

**THE GUILT OF YOUR PAST**

Guilt and regret about past actions and behaviors do not help you look or feel your best. In fact, because of that guilt, you aren't fully enjoying your current life!

Whether it is guilt about letting go of something in your closet on which you spent too much money, or guilt about a past relationship, or anything in between, you have paid enough. Guilt really is a useless emotion.

## THE PRESSURE TO PROVE YOURSELF

Slow down, choose happiness, and prioritize what is most important to you. You cannot live for other people. Stop wishing that people would see you in a certain way. Let them see who you really are. When you live for yourself, you will be happy and likely more successful anyway. You have nothing to prove. I suggest you read *Let Them* by Mel Robbins – it is life changing.

## THE WEIGHT OF OTHER'S EXPECTATIONS

Society may try to tell us what to wear, but we get to decide for ourselves. I can't control what others think, and I'm not going to change myself trying. When you stop wearing the weight of other people's expectations, you'll be lighter and freer. Wear the clothes you want to wear. Live the life you want to live.

Are you still committed to certain patterns of behavior because they worked for you in the past? To move forward, we must stop applying an old formula to a new level of life. Change up your formula and you will quickly see a different result!

## CONFIDENCE IS THE KEY

Over my amazing retail career I have met so many great women who did not have confidence! It is so sad since we are totally in charge of this feeling. I mention confidence in every single chapter of this book as it is the game changer in your life.

Confidence comes from appreciating your knowledge, skill and ability to achieve any goal in life. When you trust that you are capable of rising above anything in life, you are acting from your confidence and self worth. THIS is what I wish for you.

> **FASHION IS ABOUT DRESSING ACCORDING TO WHAT'S FASHIONABLE. STYLE IS MORE ABOUT BEING YOURSELF.**
>
> ~ OSCAR DE LA RENTA

Chapter 13

# How To Fall In Love With Yourself

OK – really? How in the world do I do that? Every once in a while I get down on myself. So I take these steps to **fall in love with myself**. It not only helps my mental health, but it also allows me to pursue my life and my passion whole-heartedly! Here are the best ways to love yourself again.

## Use Positive Affirmations

I *love* affirmations. They make me feel good! Start your day off by writing down ten positive affirmations. You can even write down ten things you love about yourself! This is a powerful way to start your day on a positive note and to reflect on the things you love about yourself. My favorites are:

- I am strong.
- I am smart.
- I am worthy.
- I am beautiful, inside and out.
- I can do anything I set my mind to.

## Appreciate, Never Compare

Sometimes we look at someone else and say, "Wow, I wish I was as thin or as pretty as she is," or "Wow, I wish I had a house or a car like that." But comparison steals your peace and happiness. It is so easy to accidentally do it without even realizing it. In those moments there is a powerful shift that you can make. Look at the beauty, or outfit, or possession of another woman and appreciate it. Enjoy it. Feel as if it was yours. Imagine how it will feel when that attribute or item *is* yours. This sends a message to the universe that can bring it to you! Like attracts like.

## Do Things You Love

When you do things you love, you will feel good about yourself. I love to style women, and I love spending time with amazing women. So I go to my store and *fill my cup* by doing these things. I love to play tennis! It's fun and I have met an entire new group of friends that I just adore. (I also love to wear all the cute outfits!) Recently I have discovered that I love to go to lunch with friends. It is so much fun to just sit and talk and eat great food!

What do you love to do? What is your passion? There's nothing as amazing as doing something about which you are passionate – something that brings you joy and fulfillment. Women are often expected to fulfill multiple roles and responsibilities, including being a wife, mother, daughter, friend, and employee. As women we need to remember that our happiness and fulfillment should not be overlooked or put on hold.

## Take Yourself Out on a Date

I am a huge fan of self care but never practiced it myself. It is a skill you can learn. I was always too busy taking care of everyone else in my life. I learned that you can do both! I am accustomed to eating by myself, as I spent many years traveling to stores. I had to learn to love myself and love spending time with myself, and you can too. Here are some dates you can do solo:

- go to the spa and just relax

- go to the gym – you will always feel better
- go to the beach or pool
- read a good novel
- go for a nice long walk – put your bare feet in the grass
- go out to eat – sit at the bar
- see a movie – you get *all* the popcorn

Give it a try. Who better to spend time with than your awesome self?

## Release Limiting Beliefs

When I retired I was bored to death. I went from working 80 hours a week to doing absolutely nothing! I would say things like, "I wonder if I will ever be successful again?" or "Will I ever find something that I love again?" The more I repeated these things the more I believed them. I needed a purpose. I still loved fashion, so I opened my own boutique: **Shecanlove** in Naples, Florida, or Shecanlove.com. It is *luxury you live in*. The boutique has workout wear, Athleisure, and great fashion. I can dress you for *every* occasion. I serve Rosé all day, and spoil and delight my clients. They mean the world to me!

Believing in myself and in my abilities was a complete game changer. I started going after my dream of working for myself, and having my own boutique. Now I get to do it ***my way***! I encourage *you* to find your purpose, change your mindset, and rework your thinking. You truly are what you *think* you are!

## Celebrate Your Wins

This one is ***huge!*** It's easy to feel like we aren't making any progress, and it can feel defeating. But, when we take a step back and celebrate the progress we've made, it is rewarding. I love to act as my own cheerleader. I do it quietly and humbly – but it works! Every step of the way is worth celebrating.

## Journal

I am ***not*** great at this yet, but I'm working on making it a habit at the end of each day. Journaling can really help you reconnect with yourself. It also brings out those inner thoughts that may hold you back, or block you from loving yourself completely. It is great to get things off your chest so you can move on – and also, to write down your wins and celebrate!

## Do Something New

Have you ever wanted to try something new but fear held you back? It's time to become **fearless** (I just *love* that word.) There is something empowering about facing your fears and overcoming them. I had a life coach early in my career who often said, "If you're not squirming you're not learning!" He challenged me every day to be a better learner and leader. He really pushed me. At the time I didn't like it; but today I see how he helped me in my career – and even more so in life. I am currently trying meditation. I really suck at sitting still; but I am working on it every day – and I'm going to **nail** it! (I'll save that for my next book.)

## Create Healthy Habits

At age 65, I can say that my habits are **really** healthy! I eat well, don't drink alcohol, and exercise regularly. Do I love going to the gym? No. But I do it because I want to look great, and it's good for my bones to create muscle. I have to push myself to drink more water. I recently made the biggest sacrifice. I gave up diet coke! I just **love** my diet coke; but everything I read tells me it is not good for me, so I just quit. All of these habits and changes in my daily routine make a huge difference when it comes to my mental health and feeling happier each day.

It takes a level of self love, dedication and determination to live your greatest life. So, look within. Look at every area of your life and ask yourself these questions: Am I on course? Am I growing mentally, emotionally and spiritually? Anything that is blocking you or preventing you from living your greatest life, ***let it go***!

> **WHOEVER SAID MONEY CAN'T BUY HAPPINESS, SIMPLY DID NOT KNOW WHERE TO SHOP.**
>
> ~ BO DEREK

# Conclusion

Well ladies, there you have it: all of my tips and tricks from 40+ years of styling women across the country. I hope that you have found this step by step guide to creating a personal style to be helpful. I hope that you will look in the mirror and smile because you look and feel beautiful!

Remember that beauty is about all of you, including: the way you carry yourself, your scent, your style, the clothes you choose, the way you interact with others, your smile. If you learn and master the tips in this book, you are bound to look and feel better every single day.

I hope you will learn as much as possible about fashion and what looks great on you. Knowledge equips you every time. The devil is in the details. I know I have given you a **lot** to process. Take baby steps. Only do what feels good and natural first, and then dare yourself to start risking some small steps. While learning to look great every day, always give room for creativity and uniqueness in whatever you wear. You don't always need to play by the rules. Most of the fashion trends that exist today were products of people's attempts to be creative, spontaneous, and innovative; and for that to have happened, some rules had to be broken. So learn to be different!

Remember, **be you!** Experiment with clothes, and find your signature style. Highlight your best features. I truly hope you found this book to be practical and useful. Never forget: *you are beautiful, and deserve to love yourself completely.*

**And remember ladies: Confidence . . . it's the single most beautiful thing a woman can wear every day.**

# Acknowledgements

I want to thank so many women who have supported me so completely in my life and in my career: my amazing family; ***all*** the women who have worked with me; the ***best*** leader and my dearest friend, Mori MacKenzie; and April O'Leary and Heather Desrocher, my publisher and editor at O'Leary Publishing, who put all my thoughts and words together to make this book magical!

# About the Author

Sher Canada is a leader and dynamic force in women's fashion. As the former Group Sr. Vice President for Chico's, Soma Intimates, and Boston Proper, she led with vision and heart, overseeing $1.9 billion in revenue. Her career also included time with **Brooks Fashions, The Limited, and The Wet Seal.** Her mantra, "Confidence . . . it's the single most beautiful thing a woman can wear every day," is woven throughout everything she does.

Sher is the founder of **Shecanlove**, a vibrant boutique in Naples, Florida, where she continues to inspire women through curated fashion and purpose-driven mission work. Sher partners with Path to Freedom to support survivors of sex trafficking – raising awareness, funds, and most importantly, hope.

With unstoppable energy, a signature sense of style, and a heart for empowering women, Sher is here to teach, love, inspire and remind every woman that she was born to lead boldly and live fully.

www.ingramcontent.com/pod-product-compliance
Lightning Source LLC
Chambersburg PA
CBHW061808070526
44586CB00024B/2765